Healthy Plates

VEGETABLES

VALERIE BODDEN

Published by Creative Education and Creative Paperbacks | P.O. Box 227, Mankato, Minnesota 56002
Creative Education and Creative Paperbacks are imprints of The Creative Company
www.thecreativecompany.us

Design by Liddy Walseth | Production by Christine Vanderbeek
Printed in the United States of America

Photographs by Alamy (PhotoAlto sas, Shotshop GmbH), Corbis (Eising Studio-Food Photo &
Video/the food passionates, Richard T. Nowitz, Jeremy Woodhouse/Blend Images), Dreamstime
(Yen Hung Lin), iStockphoto (adlifemarketing, Azurita, Devonyu, michaelgatewood, tycoon751),
Shutterstock (Andrey_Kuzmin, Jacek Chabraszewski, Pavel Hlystov, indigolotos, IriGri, Majesticca,
Alexander Pekour)

Library of Congress Cataloging-in-Publication Data
Bodden, Valerie. | Vegetables / Valerie Bodden. | p. cm. — (Healthy plates) | Summary: An early
reader's introduction to the connections between the vegetables food group and staying healthy,
benefits of vegetables such as carrots, nutritional concepts such as potassium, and recipe instruc-
tions. | Includes bibliographical references and index. | ISBN 978-1-60818-512-2 (hardcover) ISBN
978-1-62832-112-8 (pbk) | 1. Vegetables in human nutrition—Juvenile literature. I. Title.
QP144.V44B63 2015 | 613.2—dc23 | 2014000712

CCSS: RI.1.1, 2, 4, 5, 6, 7; RI.2.2, 5, 6, 7, 10; RI.3.1, 5, 7, 8; RF.1.1, 3, 4; RF.2.3, 4

First Edition 9 8 7 6 5 4 3 2 1

TABLE OF CONTENTS

Growing Up

Your body needs food to give it energy and help it grow. But not all foods are good for you. Healthy foods contain the **nutrients** (*NOO-tree-unts*) your body needs to be at its best. Healthy foods are put into five food groups: dairy, fruits, **grains**, **proteins**, and vegetables. Your body needs foods from each food group every day.

Vegetable Group

Vegetables are parts of plants that can be eaten. Vegetables give your body nutrients called carbohydrates (*kar-bo-HI-drates*). Carbohydrates give you energy.

TOMATOES ARE THE FRUITS OF PLANTS, BUT THEY ARE EATEN AS VEGGIES.

Most vegetables have fiber to keep your **digestive system** healthy. Corn and carrots have a lot of fiber. So do green beans and broccoli.

HALF A CUP OF MIXED VEGGIES HAS 16 PERCENT OF THE FIBER YOU NEED IN A DAY.

Vitamins and Nutrients

Vegetables have many **vitamins**, too. Corn, squash, and peas have B vitamins. This group of vitamins helps your body use energy from foods.

COOKS CALL SQUASH VEGGIES. PEOPLE WHO STUDY PLANTS CALL THEM FRUITS.

Broccoli, potatoes, and red and yellow peppers have Vitamin C. Vitamin C helps heal cuts and makes your body strong to fight off sicknesses. Your body gets Vitamin A from carrots, sweet potatoes, and broccoli. This vitamin gives you good eyesight.

OTHER VEGGIES LIKE RED BELL PEPPERS HAVE A LOT OF VITAMIN A, TOO.

Potatoes, green beans, and other vegetables have potassium. Potassium helps keep your **blood pressure** low. Low blood pressure keeps your heart from pumping too hard.

MANY GREEN BEANS GROW ON SMALL BUSHES. THE BEANS ARE INSIDE PODS.

How Much?

Most kids should eat about one to two cups (237–473 ml) of vegetables every day. Twelve baby carrots or one baked sweet potato make one cup of

vegetables. Two cups (473 ml) of lettuce counts as one cup of other vegetables. People who are older or more active can eat more vegetables.

Healthy Living

It is easy to eat plenty of vegetables. Munch on cucumber slices for a snack. Top your pizza with onions and peppers. Try a carrot muffin for dessert.

Eating vegetables is part of being healthy. Exercising is another part. Try to move your body an hour every day. Exercising and eating healthy can be fun—and can make you feel good, too!

STRETCHING AND RIDING YOUR BIKE HELP KEEP YOUR BODY IN SHAPE.

MAKE A VEGETABLE SNACK:

CUCUMBER SANDWICHES

4 SLICES CUCUMBER
1 SLICE BREAD
2 TBSP. CREAM CHEESE
SHREDDED CARROT

Have a grown-up help you cut the slice of bread into four pieces. Spread a thin layer of cream cheese on each slice. Top each with a slice of cucumber and a few pieces of shredded carrot. Enjoy your healthy vegetable snack!

GLOSSARY

blood pressure—how hard a person's blood pushes against the blood vessels, or tubes that carry blood through the body

digestive system—the parts of your body used in breaking down food and getting rid of waste

grains—parts of some kinds of grasses, such as wheat or oats, that are used to make bread and other foods

nutrients—the parts of food that your body uses to make energy, grow, and stay healthy

proteins—foods such as meat and nuts that contain the nutrient protein, which helps the body grow

vitamins—nutrients found in foods that are needed to keep your body healthy and working well

READ MORE

Head, Honor. *Healthy Eating*. Mankato, Minn.: Sea-to-Sea, 2013.

Kalz, Jill. *Vegetables*. North Mankato, Minn.: Smart Apple Media, 2004.

Llewellyn, Claire. *Healthy Eating*. Laguna Hills, Calif.: QEB, 2006.

WEBSITES

My Plate Kids' Place
http://www.choosemyplate.gov/kids/index.html
Check out games, activities, and recipes about eating healthy.

PBS Kids: Healthy Eating Games
http://pbskids.org/games/healthyeating.html
Play games that help you learn about healthy foods.

Note: Every effort has been made to ensure that the websites listed above are suitable for children, that they have educational value, and that they contain no inappropriate material. However, because of the nature of the Internet, it is impossible to guarantee that these sites will remain active indefinitely or that their contents will not be altered.

INDEX